The Gold Frog Hunt

By Cameron Macintosh

Holt and Quin went into the wild to find a gold frog.

"Do you mind if I bring Ben?" said Holt.

"He can come," said Quin. "But he can't bolt into the woods!"

Ben does not bolt.
He stops for a nap!

Quin scolded Holt.

“We will not find a gold frog if we stop,” she said.

Holt pats his old dog.

“Let’s find that gold frog, Ben,” said Holt.

Holt and Quin spot a colt in a field.

But Quin didn't want to see other wildlife.

Holt and Quin find some baby robins in a nest.

Holt and Quin find the robin mum on an old post.

"We can't find a gold frog!" said Quin.
"We have looked all through the woods!"

"Look behind you!" said Holt.

"Hold on, Quin!" said Holt.

"A gold frog is **on** you!"

What a bold frog!

CHECKING FOR MEANING

1. What did Quin and Holt find first? *(Literal)*
2. Where did Holt and Quin see the robin mum? *(Literal)*
3. Did Holt enjoy the walk? How do you know? *(Inferential)*
4. What could Quin have done differently to have a more fun time on the walk? *(Evaluative)*

EXTENDING VOCABULARY

bolt	If you bolt, do you move quickly or slowly?
scolded	When Quin scolded Holt, what was she doing? Have you ever been scolded?
rind	What fruits have a rind? What do we call the coverings on other fruits and vegetables?

MOVING BEYOND THE TEXT

1. What does a frog's skin look like? What does it feel like?
2. Frogs start off as eggs. What do you know about the life cycle of frogs?
3. What else might Holt and Quin have seen in the wild?
4. Should you touch a wild animal, like a frog? Why?

TIME TO WRITE

Write about going on a hunt for an animal you would like to see in the wild.